"WHY DO WE NEED ANOTHER BABY?"

Copyright © 1996 by Cynthia MacGregor

A Lyle Stuart Book
Published by Carol Publishing Group
Lyle Stuart is a registered trademark of Carol Communications, Inc.

Editorial Offices: 600 Madison Avenue, New York, N.Y. 10022
Sales and Distribution Offices: 120 Enterprise Avenue, Secaucus, N.J. 07094
In Canada: Canadian Manda Group, One Atlantic Avenue, Suite 105, Toronto,
   Ontario M6K 3E7
Queries regarding rights and permissions should be addressed to
   Carol Publishing Group, 600 Madison Avenue, New York, N.Y. 10022

Carol Publishing Group books are available at special discounts for bulk purchases, sales promotion, fund-raising, or educational purposes. Special editions can be created to specifications. For details contact: Special Sales Department, Carol Publishing Group, 120 Enterprise Avenue, Secaucus, N.J. 07094

Manufactured in the United States of America

10   9   8   7   6   5   4   3   2   1

Library of Congress Cataloging-in-Publication Data

MacGregor, Cynthia.
    Why do we need another baby?" : helping your child welcome a new
arrival, with love and illustrations / Cynthia MacGregor ;
illustrations by David Clark.
       p.   cm.
    "A Lyle Stuart book."
    ISBN 0–8184–0578–3 (hardcover)
    1. Sibling rivalry,.   2. Jealousy in children.   3. Child rearing.
I. Clark, David, 1960–   . II. Title.
B723.S43M33   1996
649′.143—dc20
                                                    95–50097
                                                       CIP

"WHY DO WE NEED ANOTHER BABY?"

Helping your child welcome a new arrival—with love and illustrations

CYNTHIA MacGREGOR
ILLUSTRATIONS BY DAVID CLARK

Published by Carol Publishing Group

Do things seem a little different around your house lately? Maybe you've noticed that your mommy looks a little rounder. Or even a lot rounder. You may think she looks like she swallowed a balloon. (Of course you know your mommy wouldn't really do anything that silly!)

Hmm... what's going on around here?

"*My* doctor listens to my *chest*."

There may be other unusual things going on—signs that something important and exciting is happening. For instance, you may have noticed that Mom is going to the doctor more often. She doesn't have the chicken pox or an earache. But even though she says she's fine, she keeps going back to the doctor.

Maybe your doctor gives you a lollypop after every visit, but Mommy's doctor doesn't. If she's not sick, and she's not going there to get lollypops, she must just be getting a checkup. But why does she need so many checkups? And what does it have to do with her looking so round?

Do you want to know what this is all about? I'm going to tell you.

One of the happiest days in your parents' life was a day that was very special to you, too, even though you don't remember it. I'm talking about the day you were born.

Your birthday celebrates the day you were born—the day that you became a part of this world. On that day your mom and dad held you in their arms for the first time.

Your mom and dad waited nine months for you. That's how long it takes a baby to grow inside its mommy's body.

A baby starts growing in a special place inside its mom's tummy, called the womb. That's pronounced "woom" to rhyme with "room," and it is sort of like a little room. It's the baby's own little room inside Mommy, where the baby stays while it's growing big enough to be born and come out into the world.

The womb is a snug, cozy, comfy little place inside a woman's tummy. A baby lives there for the first nine months, until he or she gets born.

It's not the same place where Mommy's food goes after she eats. It would be pretty messy if the baby were rolling around in tuna fish or alphabet soup. But the baby doesn't have to do that! The womb is a separate place, not connected to where the food goes.

After the baby grows for nine months in Mommy's womb, the baby is ready to be born. That means it comes out into the world. You don't remember the first time you saw your parents, but they'll never forget the first time they saw you.

When a baby is born, the parents are very happy. They've waited a long time for this day. When you were inside your mom's womb, she couldn't see you or hold you or hug you. She and your dad couldn't do all the fun things they do with you now. Or show you how much they love you. When a baby is born, it's a very exciting time. It's the beginning of a family.

It's the start of a lot of enjoyment. And a lot of love. Your parents love you very much. You know that, right? And they like to spend time with you and do things with you. They like to sing to you, bathe you, tell you stories, and all kinds of other fun stuff. That's what families do together.

Being the parents in a family is a serious responsibility, but it's also a wonderful feeling.

It's so wonderful, in fact, that your mom and dad decided they wanted an even bigger family. Another child to have fun with, to love. Another child to cuddle, to play with, to enjoy.

This new child will be very special to you, too. This new child will be your little brother or sister.

Of course, your new brother or sister won't be able to play ball or building blocks with you right away. Your new brother or sister starts out life as a baby. Just like you did. Just like everyone does. And when did you ever see a baby jump rope or ride a tricycle? Babies can't even walk!

Babies are great at sleeping but no good at games.

At first he or she will mostly sleep, cry, and drink milk. Babies are sweet and cute, but they aren't much fun in the beginning. They can't talk or sing. They can't play catch. They can't get into contests to see who can come out with the loudest, most gross burp, or who can make the ugliest, funniest, most scrunched up face.

What babies do best is gurgle and cry and wet their diapers. None of that sounds like much fun to a big kid like you, does it?

"Hmm. I'm not sure we really need this new baby around here."

But babies grow. You were a baby once—not that many years ago. And look at you now! In a few years, your new baby brother or sister will be a kid old enough for you to play with and have fun with. And he or she will look up to you because you're older and smarter.

You'll be better at throwing a ball and at reading books. You'll know the rules of lots of games, and where the best hiding places are for Hide and Seek, and all kinds of other Important Stuff.

You'll be a Very Important Person to your younger brother or sister. And the two of you can have lots of fun together.

"If my parents love me so much, why do they need another child?"

If you have a pet dog or turtle, I'll bet you love it. But I'll bet maybe you've asked Mom and Dad for another dog or turtle or cat or hamster. You have enough love in you to love two or three or four guinea pigs, or two or three or four goldfish. And if you get another dog, it doesn't mean you don't love the first dog anymore. You won't love your first dog any <u>less</u> if you get a new dog either.

In fact, it's just because you love your dog so much that you think it would be really neat to have two. And if you already have two dogs, I'll bet you're begging Mom and Dad for a third dog! Right?!

Lots of love to share!

If you don't have any brothers or sisters, you're probably thinking, "Right now, I get all of Mommy and Daddy's love. When there's a new baby around, I'll have to share that love."

And if you've already got a sister or a brother, you're probably thinking, "I have to share Mommy and Daddy now. When the new baby is born, I'll have to share their love even more."

But that's not true.

Love isn't like apple pie. If I give you an apple pie and tell you that you may eat it all, you have a whole pie for yourself, right? (Although I hope you wouldn't eat it all at once, or you might wind up feeling kind of sick in your stomach.)

But if I tell you to share the pie with your best friend, your friend gets some of the pie ...and then there's less pie left for you.

Love isn't like that. Love is something parents never run out of. Your parents will love the new baby for sure, but they'll still love you just as much as ever. Having the new baby around will remind them of how cute you were when you were a baby. And how tiny. And how sweet.

So they won't love you any less than they do now. And they might appreciate you even more, because you're big enough to talk to and be a helper.

Your parents have lots and lots of love to give. No matter how much Mommy and Daddy love the new baby, they will keep loving you very, very much every day.

Because now you're extra special to them. Your their _big_ girl or boy. You can even be Mom and Dad's helper and help with the baby.

But even though you'll be just as important to Mom and Dad as you've always been, you _will_ have to share their time. Babies need a lot of attention. Babies get hungry and want to drink milk. Babies need their diapers changed. Babies need to be held.

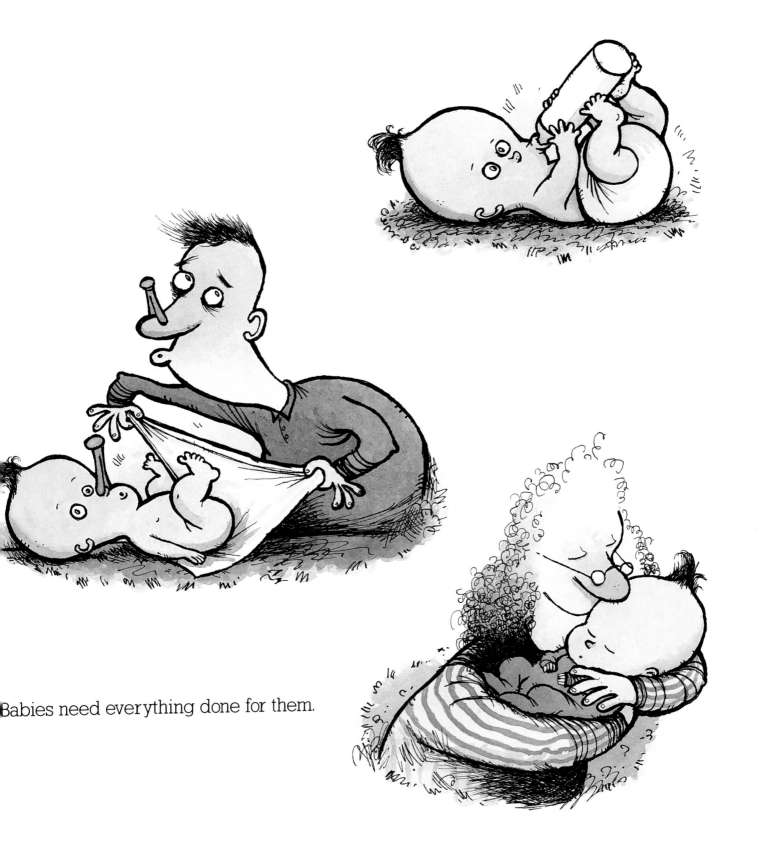

Babies need everything done for them.

"I can help, too!"

I'll bet you like to be held, too. Well, Mommy and Daddy will still have time to hold you. But they'll also need to hold the baby.

But you know what else? They'll let <u>you</u> hold the baby, too.

You'll have to share Mommy and Daddy with the baby, but here's a little secret: Mommy and Daddy will be sharing the baby with you.

Yes, <u>you</u>!

Your mommy and daddy will be the new baby's mommy and daddy, too. Of course. But you're going to be someone very important to the baby, too.

If you're a boy, you're going to be the baby's brother. And if you're a girl, you're going to be the baby's sister.

The <u>older</u> brother or <u>older</u> sister. And that's a very important thing to be. You see, this isn't just Mommy and Daddy's new baby. It's your new baby, too.

Sometimes parents find out before the baby is born whether it's going to be a boy or a girl. Sometimes they don't know until it's born.

Surprise!

Your parents may already know whether you're going to get a baby brother or a baby sister. If they don't know yet, maybe the doctor will be able to tell them soon. Or maybe they won't know until the baby is born.

"I'd like to have a baby brother, please."

In any case, it's <u>not</u> like going to a restaurant. You can't order what you want and get it. "Doctor, I want a boy this time," or "Doctor, I want a girl this time." It doesn't work like that.

Let's say you especially want a baby brother, or a baby sister. There's no point in asking your parents for the one you want, because they can't do anything about it. And neither can you.

Now let's talk some more about this baby. This new little kid who's going to be living in your house.

At first the baby isn't going to do much or be much fun for you. But when he or she is around one year old, your younger brother or sister will learn to walk. Pretty soon, he or she will start talking. And before long, that baby won't be a baby anymore. He or she will be a little girl or boy. Kind of like you are now.

And you'll be bigger. You'll always be the baby's older brother or sister.

Babies crawl, then learn to walk.

They babble, then they learn to talk.

You'll always be a step (or two) ahead of him or her.

Because you're older, you'll probably have more privileges. This means you'll have permission to stay up later than your brother or sister and permission to do other things your brother or sister isn't allowed to do yet. You'll be allowed to cross the street by yourself before he or she is, and you'll ride a two-wheeler while he or she still rides a tricycle. You'll be in the school for big kids and you'll know more stuff, 'cause you're older.

If you have an older brother or sister, probably he or she gets to do some neat stuff that you don't get to do. Do you sometimes feel bad? Do you ever feel left out when he or she stays up later than you or gets to do other things you can't?

Well, now it's going to be <u>your</u> turn to be the big kid, the one with all the privileges. Your older brother or sister will always be ahead of you, but you'll always be ahead of the new baby. Now you'll be the one who gets to do grown-up kinds of things, while he or she isn't allowed, and you'll sit in a real chair at the dining table instead of a high chair or booster seat, and you'll choose what clothes you're going to put on in the mornings, all by yourself.

Being older gives
you lots of privileges.

It's fun to know you have more privileges than your younger brother or sister. But that certainly isn't the only way you're going to enjoy the new baby.

For instance, the baby will be someone for you to play with.

When the baby is first born, of course, and for quite a while after that, he or she will be too young to play games. How can a baby play Go Fish! when he or she can't even talk? That's silly!

But as soon as the baby is born, you can play This Little Piggy with the baby's toes. You can sing to the baby. You can hold the baby in your lap.

"This little piggy went to market."

And when the baby gets older, you'll have a brother or sister to play with for real. You can play Tag and Hide and Seek and lots of other games.

"One, two, four, eight..."

As you and the baby both get older, you'll be able to read to him or her. Just the way Mommy and Daddy read to you now. You can tell the baby stories. You can answer questions. Your younger brother or sister will look up to you—that means he or she will think you're really great!

And you know what? Your brother or sister will be very important to you, too.

Here's some more fun you can have with him or her:

You can tell each other scary stories.

You can whisper secrets in the dark.

You can squirt each other with water pistols and splash each other in the tub.

You can make noise together.

You can make music together, singing, or playing the drums, or the piano, or the toy tambourine or triangle.

And you can hold each other at night if you hear a noise and get scared.

If you already have a brother or sister, now you'll have another one. Another one to play with, to share secrets with, to make plans with, to enjoy being with. And if you're now an "only" child, you will have all that fun and enjoyment for the first time. You'll have a built-in friend, someone to play with or talk to when your friends aren't around and Mommy and Daddy are too busy.

As you grow older, you make new friends. But sometimes friends move. They don't live in your town or city anymore. And you can't play with them anymore.

A brother or sister is a friend who will never move away from you. At least, not until you're grown up.

Friends sometimes move away. Brothers and sisters will still be around.

Your younger brother or sister will look up to you and depend on you. You can help him or her get dressed, help him or her learn how to play games, show him or her how to build towers out of blocks and even how to ride a bike when you're both older.

Your little brother or sister will love you and depend on you. He or she will think you're very special and really important.

(And he or she will be right. You <u>will</u> be special and important. To your brother or sister, and to Mommy and Daddy, too.)

So, now you know what's going on in your family these days and what's going to be happening soon. It's pretty exciting, isn't it?

Your mom and dad can't tell you exactly when the baby's going to be born. But they have a good idea of approximately when it will happen.

Your mom will probably go to the hospital when she feels the baby getting ready to be born. Most babies are born in hospitals. And when she comes home, she'll have the baby with her.

Hurry! It's time for the baby!

Congratulations! You're going to be an Older Brother or an Older Sister. And that's a very important thing to be!

You should feel very special now!